# Cotswold Cy

C000001150

by
## Sheila Booth

GOOD VIEWS

WEATHER

BEAUTIFUL BARNS

PUB STOPS

PICNIC PLACES

FORDS TO CROSS

CHURCHES TO VISIT

WHITE ROADS

## ALL ON A DAY'S RIDE

### MAPS

All the rides have an excellent sketch map by Peter Reardon but if you would
like to see the routes in greater detail then we would recommend
Ordnance Survey Touring Maps "The Cotswold and Gloucestershire"
(1 inch to 1.6 miles: 1 cm to 1 km)
Ordnance Survey Explorer OL45 "The Cotswolds"
(2 1/2 inches to 1 mile: 4 cm = 1 km)

Published
by
**REARDON PUBLISHING**
56, Upper Norwood Street
Cheltenham, GL53 0DU
England
www.reardon.co.uk
Email: reardon@bigfoot.com

Written and Researched
by
Sheila Booth

**ISBN 1 873877 60 9**

Design and Layout
by
Nicholas Reardon

Maps and Illustrations
by
Peter T Reardon

Photographs by Nicholas Reardon
Front cover: Lower Slaughter
Inside front: Cotswolds at Dusk
Inside back: Cotswold Trees
Back cover: Bike at rest Coopers Hill

Printed
in
Cheltenham

# Introduction

This book of Cotswold cycle rides is designed particularly for those who like country pubs, but the rides can be enjoyed by everyone who enjoys short rides in the countryside.

The rides are between 10 and 16 miles long, and all can be ridden in an afternoon, a morning or on a summer's evening. They are mainly on quiet country roads, though some cross classified roads or have a short stretch along one; one or two rides have a short stretch on a bridle path.

There are three easy - flattish - rides, two near the River Severn and one near the Cotswold Water Park. The moderate rides have some longish or steepish hills, but most people should find them fairly easy even though they may need to walk a short stretch. The strenuous rides have some long and/or steep hills - and of course they also have some downhills!

## What to wear and take with you

It is not necessary to buy specialised cycling clothes, but is is sensible to wear bright clothing so that car drivers can see you easily. It is a good idea to wear shorts, or trousers which are easy to move in but fairly close to the leg below the knee - leggings are ideal - this stops your trousers catching the chain. If you haven't got narrow legged trousers a rubber band will hold them in. Wear shoes with a firm, flat sole so that you will be able to press down on the pedals easily, and perhaps take a warm jacket, and something waterproof. Gloves keep your hands warm and protect them;  a helmet is not a legal requirement, but gives protection to your head if you fall.

Carry a pump, a spare inner tube, lights, a small tool kit, something to eat - chocolate, bananas - and a small first aid kit. Pack items that you are carrying carefully - loose items can be dangerous.

* * * *

Check your cycle over before you set out and make sure that the brakes, gears, etc are working properly and that your tyres are blown up. Always obey the Highway Code, and ride in single file on narrow or busy roads. Some roads have poor surfaces, so watch out for potholes and poor edges to the roads, and warn the other riders about them.

We hope you enjoy the rides. The information contained in these rides is believed to be accurate but the author accepts no responsibility for difficulties, delays, accidents, loss, etc., as a result of cycle rides based on information herein.

# RANGEWORTHY, TWO COMMONS AND WICKWAR

**Distance: 14 miles / 22.4 km    Terrain ** moderate**

This is an undulating ride on quiet lanes, some of which are part of the Avon Cycleway. In general the route is flat particularly over the commons, but there are a few hills. The pubs are both in the north west part of the ride, and on a warm day a picnic on either of the commons would be pleasant. There is part of the route which has an alternative along a bridlepath, but beware if there has been rain!

In Rangeworthy go south on B4058 and just outside the village turn left along Manor Road - unsigned. At the junction after 0.6m (#) turn left along Tanhouse Lane signed Yate Rocks. Go up the hill, keeping left at junction signed Wickwar, to B4060. [2.7m/4.3km]

Straight over B4060 along Mapleridge Lane, and at junction after 1.5m turn left into Horton. Turn left in Horton opposite the Social Club along King Lane signed Hawkesbury, and follow the road to the cattlegrid onto Hawkesbury Common. [3.7m/5.9km]*or Straight over B4060 along Mapleridge Lane, and after 0.3m turn left up signed bridlepath. At the gates to Lady's Wood House keep left up the bridlepath which goes round the edge of the wood. The path is used by horses, and in parts it is rather uneven - give way to horses along here. The path becomes a track again and then a tarmacked road - Vinney Lane which leads to T jn. Turn left here (no sign), and follow the road to the cattle grid onto Hawkesbury Common. [3.3m/5.3km]*

Straight over Hawkesbury Common to a junction and turn left opposite the 'phone box signed Wickwar. The road goes over Inglestone Common, and down and up a steepish hill to the B4060 in Wickwar. [3.6m/5.8km]

Turn left up into the town signed Yate and follow the road up to the left to the PH. From the PH start coming back down the hill, but immediately turn left along The Downs (B4509) signed Charfield. Take the first left turn signed Westend, and then follow this road for 0.9m to T junction. Turn right (unsigned) and back to Rangeworthy.  For the PH turn right at B4508 to the Rose and Crown on the right after 0.3m. [4m/6.4km]

## INFORMATION
**Pubs:**  Wickwar - *The Buthay* Rangeworthy - *Rose and Crown*
**Rail access:-** Yate Station is only 2 miles south of the ride - from the station cycle north past Engine Common and start the ride at (#).
**Parking**: You could park in Rangeworthy or Wickwar.
**Towns and Attractions:** see page 36 - 38.

# RANGEWORTHY, TWO COMMONS AND WICKWAR

### Distance: 14 miles / 22.4 km   Terrain ** moderate

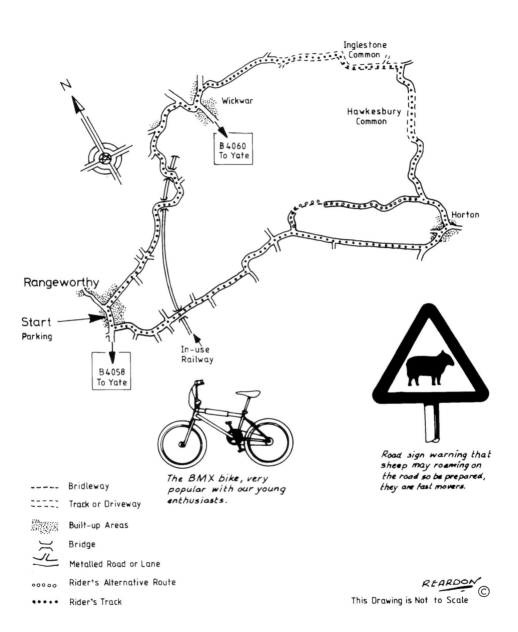

Inglestone Common

Wickwar

B4060 To Yate

Hawkesbury Common

Horton

Rangeworthy

Start
Parking

B4058 To Yate

In-use Railway

The BMX bike, very popular with our young enthusiasts.

Road sign warning that sheep may roaming on the road so be prepared, they are fast movers.

| | |
|---|---|
| ----- | Bridleway |
| ⌐⌐⌐⌐⌐ | Track or Driveway |
| ░░░ | Built-up Areas |
| ⌣⌣ | Bridge |
| ᴊᴌ | Metalled Road or Lane |
| ooooo | Rider's Alternative Route |
| ••••• | Rider's Track |

REARDON ©

This Drawing is Not to Scale

# SHERSTON, EASTON GREY AND LEIGHTERTON
## Distance: 14.5 miles / 23.2 km Terrain ** moderate

This delightful ride over gently undulating countryside is in the relatively unknown south west Cotswolds. It goes through attractive villages, and crosses the River Avon.

From Sherston (1) go down the minor road opposite the church signed Hullavington. Cross the River Avon and bear left up Bustlers Hill, and at the junction after 0.5m turn left signed Foxley. Straight over first X roads, and then after 1.3m at next X roads turn left signed Easton Grey, and down the hill to the river. [2.8m/4.5km]

Continue through Easton Grey (2) and up to B4040 X rds, and straight over signed Shipton Moyne. After 1.1m turn right signed Shipton Moyne. Turn left into Shipton Moyne signed Tetbury. [2.2m/3.5km]

Just through Shipton Moyne turn left signed Westonbirt, and at the next T junction turn right to A433. [At A433 X roads you could turn left to Westonbirt Arboretum (3), and return (+ 2m)]. Go straight over A433 signed Leighterton, and continue for 1.2m to X roads with Leighterton signed to the left; turn left to Leighterton. [5.2m/8.3km]

Turn left at the PH in Leighterton (4) and keep left and pass the church on the left, and just after the pond turn left signed Knockdown. Straight over the A433 at Knockdown signed Sherston, and back to Sherston (1). [4.3m/6.9km]

## INFORMATION

**Pubs:** Sherston - several in the town
Shipton Moyne - *Cat and Custard Pot*
Leighterton - *Royal Oak*
Knockdown on A433 - *Holford Arms*

**Parking:** You could park in Sherston.

**Towns and Attractions:** see pages 36 - 38.
(1) Sherstone, (2) Eastern Grey
(3) Westonbirt Arboretum
(4) Leighterton

# SHERSTON, EASTON GREY AND LEIGHTERTON
## Distance:  14.5 miles / 23.2 km Terrain ** moderate

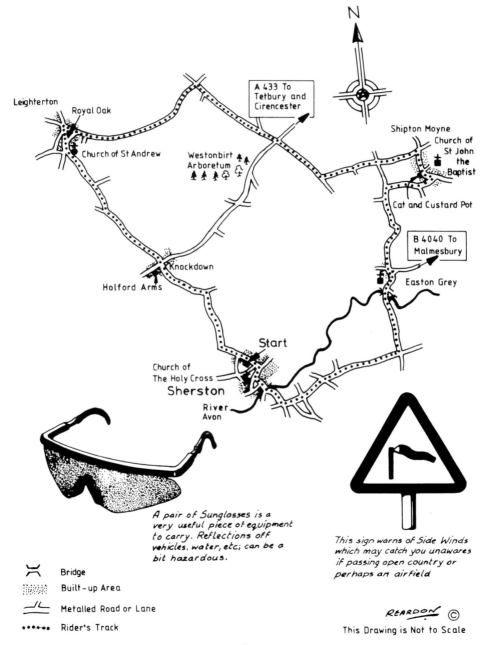

A 433 To
Tetbury and
Cirencester

N

Leighterton
Royal Oak

Church of St Andrew

Westonbirt
Arboretum

Shipton Moyne
Church of
St John
the
Baptist

Cat and Custard Pot

B 4040 To
Malmesbury

Knockdown

Holford Arms

Easton Grey

Start

Church of
The Holy Cross

Sherston

River
Avon

*A pair of Sunglasses is a
very useful piece of equipment
to carry. Reflections off
vehicles, water, etc; can be a
bit hazardous.*

*This sign warns of Side Winds
which may catch you unawares
if passing open country or
perhaps an airfield*

⌣  Bridge

▦  Built-up Area

⌒  Metalled Road or Lane

•••••  Rider's Track

REARDON ©

This Drawing is Not to Scale

# LEIGHTERTON, KINGSCOTE AND OZLEWORTH
## Distance:  15.8 miles / 25.4km  Terrain *** strenuous

This is a delightful but hilly ride in the quiet countryside near Wotton under Edge. The ride goes past Ozleworth church and along the bottom before returning through Tresham to Leighterton.

From Leighterton (4) X roads by the Royal Oak PH take the road east signed Tetbury. You will pass the American cemetery on the right. At the X roads turn left signed Dursley, and at A46 go straight over, signed Kingscote, and continue to A4135. [4.9m/7.9km]

Turn left along A4135 for 0.5m to Hunters Hall Inn. Just before the hotel turn left signed Bagpath, and follow this undulating lane to X roads. Go over, unsigned, and down a steep hill and up the other side - be particularly careful along this stretch as the road surface is poor and there is gravel in the road. At the T junction turn left, no sign, and at the next junction near Ozleworth Beacon keep left signed Newark Park, and left at next junction signed Ozleworth. After 0.4m just before the gates of Ozleworth Park the church (5) is signed to the left along a bridlepath. [3.5m/5.6km]

Keep on down the steep hill and after 0.5m the road turns sharp right near some more iron gates.  Follow the road round along the valley bottom to T junction in Wortley. Turn left here signed Hillesley, but continue only for 0.5m to Alderley. [3.1m/5km]

In Alderley turn left signed Tresham. Go straight through Tresham and up to A46. Turn left along it and immediately right signed Leighterton, and back to Leighterton. [4.3m/6.9km]


## INFORMATION

**Pubs:**  Leighterton - *Royal Oak*
Kingscote - *Hunters Hall Inn*

**Parking:**  There is very limited parking in Leighterton.

**Towns and Attractions:** see pages 36 - 38.
(4) Leighterton,
(5) Ozleworth Church

# LEIGHTERTON, KINGSCOTE AND OZLEWORTH
## Distance: 15.8 miles / 25.4km Terrain *** strenuous

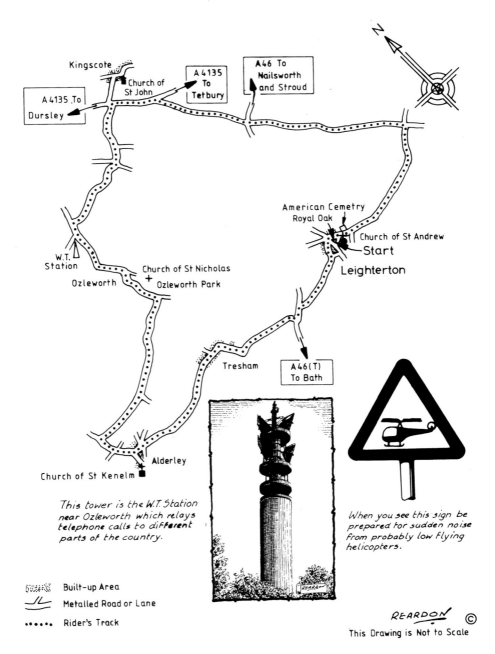

This tower is the W.T. Station near Ozleworth which relays telephone calls to different parts of the country.

When you see this sign be prepared for sudden noise from probably low flying helicopters.

Built-up Area

Metalled Road or Lane

Rider's Track

REARDON ©
This Drawing is Not to Scale

# SOUTH CERNEY, ASHTON KEYNES AND CRICKLADE
## Distance:  12.8 miles / 20.5km   Terrain * easy

This easy ride visits South Cerney and  Ashton Keynes in the Cotswold Water Park, and Cricklade. From Cricklade it follows the old railway track back to South Cerney.   The ride passes several lakes, formed as a result of gravel extraction, and now used for leisure pursuits.

From South Cerney (6) go west along Station Road and High Street and turn left down Broadway Lane near a War Memorial. Go straight over B4696 X roads along Wickwater Lane, and at the next T junction turn right - unsigned. At the next T junction turn left, and follow this road until it comes into the outskirts of Ashton Keynes (7) along Rixon Gate. Take the first right turn (Kent End), and follow this road until it bears left and becomes Back St. Pass the PH on right and continue to T junction. [4m/6.4km]

Turn left along High Road, past the War Memorial, and then parallel to the stream; and at the X roads turn left along Happy Land signed Cricklade. Continue along this road for 2.3m, and then straight over B4040 signed Chelworth. At next X roads turn left signed Cricklade. After 1.1m in Cricklade outskirts turn left at T junction and then bear right at mini-roundabout, both signed Town Centre, into Cricklade (8). [4.6m /7.4km]

Leave Cricklade along Bath Road near the clock, & pass the church on left; go through the bollards and keep straight on. Bath Road becomes Culver Hay. At T junction turn right, and first left up Stones Lane. At the next T junction turn right - the Leisure Centre will be on your left. The road bends left and soon after you have turned the corner there is a metal gate on the left (with an opening on its right hand side). Go through and follow the bridlepath/old railway track under the bridge, and over the river. The track goes under another road bridge and after another mile crosses B4696 - with care  [(#) there is a Water Park parking place here]. After another 0.5m bear right through gate, and turn left along road back into South Cerney (6). [4.2m/6.7km]

## INFORMATION

**Pubs:**  South Cerney - *Eliot Arms Hotel* in Clarks Hay, and *Royal Oak*.
Ashton Keynes - *White Hart*. Cricklade - *White Lion*
**Rail access:**   Kemble Station is 4.5 miles west of South Cerney.
**Parking:**  On the side of the road in South Cerney;
or (#) in the Water Park on the bridlepath off B4696.
**Towns and Attractions:**  see pages 36 - 38.
(6) South Cerney, (7) Aston Keynes, (8) Cricklade

# SOUTH CERNEY, ASHTON KEYNES AND CRICKLADE
## Distance:  12.8 miles / 20.5km   Terrain * easy

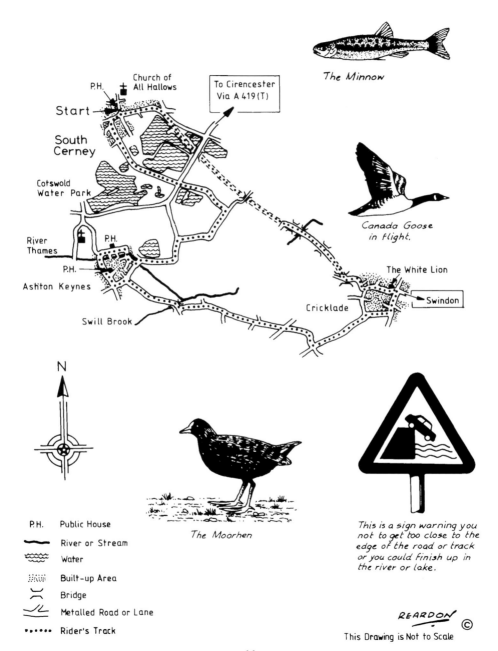

The Minnow

Canada Goose
in flight.

The Moorhen

This is a sign warning you
not to get too close to the
edge of the road or track
or you could finish up in
the river or lake.

P.H.     Public House

———     River or Stream

~~~~~    Water

▦▦▦      Built-up Area

≻≺       Bridge

～ᒋ       Metalled Road or Lane

••••••   Rider's Track

REARDON ©

This Drawing is Not to Scale

# SLIMBRIDGE, PURTON AND THE TOWPATH
## Distance:  10 miles / 16 km   Terrain * easy

This easy ride near the River Severn starts along the quiet lanes between Slimbridge and Berkeley, and returns along the Gloucester and Sharpness Canal towpath. Note that a permit is required to cycle along the towpath (#).

From the canal (9) at Shepherds Patch cycle towards Slimbridge and after 0.5m as the road bends left turn right down Lightenbrook Lane (no sign). At the T junction turn right, unsigned, and then right again at the next T junction signed Halmore. At the Halmore T junction turn left signed Wanswell and then first right signed Berkeley. [4.6m/7.4km]

At the Wanswell T junction turn right signed Brookend, and as the road turns left keep straight on signed Purton. In Purton turn left over the canal along the lane to the Berkeley Arms Inn. [2.5m/4km]

Return to the canal and turn left along it. The towpath is rather bumpy and narrow in places so ride with care. Continue for almost three miles back to the bridge at Shepherds Patch. (You might like to rest on the sculptured bench as you leave the canal. (To visit the Wildfowl Trust (10) turn left along the road +1m.)[2.9m/4.6km]


## INFORMATION

**Pubs:**  Shepherds Patch - *Tudor Arms*
Wanswell - *Salmon Inn*
Brookend - *Lammastide Inn*
Purton - *Berkeley Arms Hotel*

**Rail access:**  Cam and Dursley station is 2.4m east of the route.

**Parking:**  You could park at the side of the road at Shepherds Patch, or over the canal bridge at Purton.

(#) Canal Towpath Cycling Permit; Obtainable free from British Waterways Board, Llanthony Warehouse, Gloucester:

**Towns and Attractions:** see pages 36 - 38.
(9) Gloucester and Sharpness Canel
(10) The Wildfowl and Wetland Trust

# SLIMBRIDGE, PURTON AND THE TOWPATH
## Distance: 10 miles / 16 km   Terrain * easy

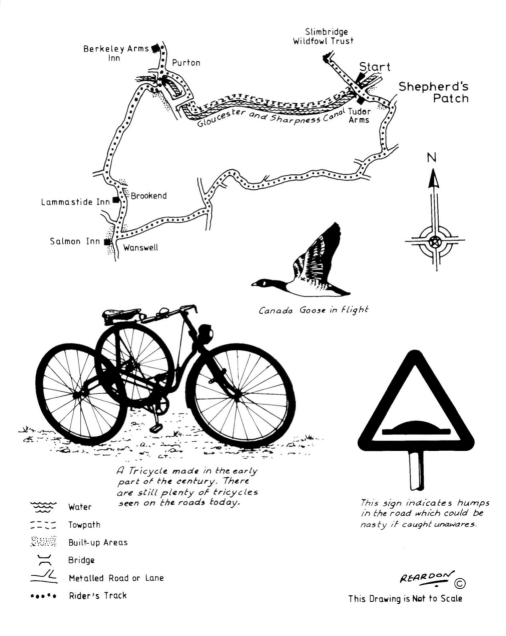

Berkeley Arms Inn

Purton

Slimbridge Wildfowl Trust

Start

Shepherd's Patch

Gloucester and Sharpness Canal

Tudor Arms

Lammastide Inn

Brookend

Salmon Inn

Wanswell

N

Canada Goose in Flight

A Tricycle made in the early part of the century. There are still plenty of tricycles seen on the roads today.

~~~~ Water

===== Towpath

Built-up Areas

Bridge

Metalled Road or Lane

•••• Rider's Track

This sign indicates humps in the road which could be nasty if caught unawares.

REARDON ©

This Drawing is Not to Scale

# FRAMPTON ON SEVERN, ARLINGHAM PASSAGE AND EPNEY
## Distance:  13.7 miles / 21.9km   Terrain * easy

This fairly easy ride goes to Arlingham Passage with its fine views over the River Severn.  It returns along the river bank to Epney, and then to Frampton on the towpath. The ride is fairly flat, but riding along the towpath is more strenuous than along the road; and you need a canal permit for the towpath (#).

From the green at Frampton (11) ride up to the B4071 and turn left and over the canal. Bear left signed Arlingham. Cycle straight through Fretherne, and then through Arlingham, signed Arlingham Passage, to the River Severn (12). [4.4m/7km]

Return on the same road through Arlingham, and after another 1.5m turn left on the brow of a hill opposite Overton Farm signed Overton Lane. The road goes along the river bank; and then keep on along the road to Saul. Turn left in Saul (13) at the T junction signed Upper Framilode; continue to Epney where the road again goes along the river bank. [6.1m/9.8km]

Turn right in Epney signed Gloucester, and continue to the Gloucester and Sharpness canal (9) at Parkend Bridge. Turn right onto the towpath before you cross the canal, and follow it through Saul Junction to the next bridge. Turn left here, and then right at the first T junction signed Frampton, and back to Frampton. [3.2m/5.1km]

## INFORMATION

**Pubs:**  Frampton on Severn - *The Three Horseshoes*, and *The Bell*
Arlingham - *Red Lion Inn*
Arlingham Passage -*The Old Passage Inn*
Framilode - *The Ship Inn*
Epney - *The Anchor*  Parkend Bridge - *The Castle*

**Rail access:**  Stonehouse station is 5 miles to the east of Frampton.

**Parking:**  You could park in Frampton.

(#) Canal Towpath Cycling Permit - obtainable free from British Waterways Board, Llanthony Warehouse, Gloucester.

**Towns and Attractions:**  see pages 36 - 38.
(9) Gloucester and Sharpness Canal,
(11) Frampton on Severn, (12) The River Severn, (13) Saul Junction

# FRAMPTON ON SEVERN, ARLINGHAM PASSAGE AND EPNEY
## Distance: 13.7 miles / 21.9km   Terrain * easy

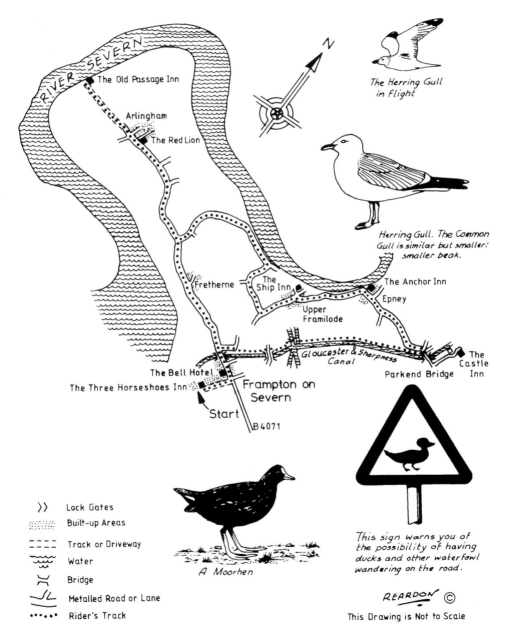

The Herring Gull
in Flight

Herring Gull. The Common
Gull is similar but smaller:
smaller beak.

This sign warns you of
the possibility of having
ducks and other waterfowl
wandering on the road.

A Moorhen

REARDON ©

This Drawing is Not to Scale

| >> | Lock Gates |
| | Built-up Areas |
| ---- | Track or Driveway |
| ~~~~ | Water |
| )( | Bridge |
| ~L | Metalled Road or Lane |
| •••••• | Rider's Track |

# MINCHINHAMPTON, CHERINGTON AND FRAMPTON MANSELL
## Distance: 13.2 miles / 21.1km   Terrain ** moderate

This ride starts in Minchinhampton, a town where the wealthy wool merchants built their houses. It then goes along the lane to Cherington, passing Cherington Lake - it is worth stopping here. The return to Minchinhampton is via Frampton Mansell, with its views over the Stroud valley.

From Minchinhampton (14) square go down to the X roads and turn left up Tetbury Street, and continue along this undulating lane for one mile past the Hampton Fields sign to a left turn at a grassy triangle signed Cherington. Straight over the immediate X roads, and then down the lane, and to Cherington Lake on the right. [2.4m/3.8km]

Continue along this lane and bear left at junction into Cherington (15). Turn left in the village opposite the green signed Rodmarton. As you leave the village turn left signed Sapperton; then over the first X roads and over A419 both signed Sapperton. [4.6m/7.4km]

At the next X roads go straight over signed Sapperton, and then left into Sapperton village (16). Follow the road through the  village and then straight over the X roads signed Frampton Mansell, and continue along this lane to Frampton Mansell. [2.4m/3.8km]

Straight through Frampton Mansell to A419, and turn right along it with care, opposite the White Horse PH.  After 0.7m turn left signed Minchinhampton, and as you get to the town turn left signed Minchinhampton and back to the centre. [3.8m/6.1km]

## INFORMATION

**Pubs:**   Minchinhampton - *The Crown Inn*
Sapperton - *The Bell Inn*
Frampton Mansell - *The Crown Inn*
A419 - *The White Horse*

**Rail access:**   The nearest station is at Stroud.

**Parking:**  There is some parking in Minchinhampton.

**Towns and Attractions:** see pages 36 - 38.
(14) Minchinhampton, (15) Cherington,
(16) Sapperton

# MINCHINHAMPTON, CHERINGTON AND FRAMPTON MANSELL
## Distance: 13.2 miles / 21.1km   Terrain ** moderate

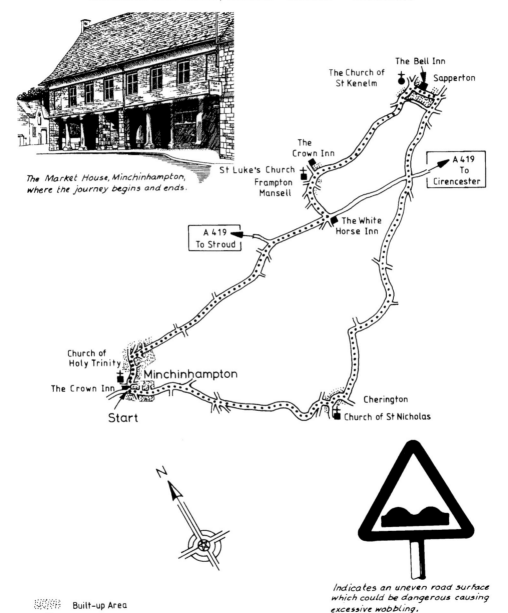

*The Market House, Minchinhampton, where the journey begins and ends.*

The Bell Inn

The Church of St Kenelm

Sapperton

The Crown Inn

St Luke's Church

Frampton Mansell

A 419 To Cirencester

The White Horse Inn

A 419 To Stroud

Church of Holy Trinity

Minchinhampton

The Crown Inn

Start

Cherington

Church of St Nicholas

N

*Indicates an uneven road surface which could be dangerous causing excessive wobbling.*

REARDON ©

This Drawing is Not to Scale

Built-up Area

Metalled Road or Lane

Rider's Track

- 17 -

# BISLEY, MISERDEN AND DANEWAY
## Distance:  12.4 miles / 19.8km  Terrain *** strenuous

This hilly ride starts in Bisley, a handsome town where the wool merchants built their houses. It goes north to The Camp and Miserden, and then swoops down-hill to Daneway. The last section of the ride is hilly.

Leave Bisley (17) to the north, with the Stirrup Cup PH on left, and follow this road for 2.5m to The Camp. At the bottom of the hill just after The Camp turn right signed Miserden, and follow this lane down, then up hill to a T junction. Turn right here, then first left, both signed Miserden, and into Miserden village (18). [4.6m/7.4km]

Turn right in Miserden and pass the PH on the right and to a T junction.  Turn left here signed Edgeworth, and follow this lane - mainly downhill - to the canal at Daneway (19). [3.8m/6km]

Take the road opposite the PH signed Bisley and follow this undulating lane for about one mile to left turn part way up a hill, signed Far Oakridge. Turn left and follow signs to Bisley for about a mile until you reach the X roads with Oakridge Lynch signed to left and Waterlane to right. Turn left here to PH just down the road on the left. [2.2m/3.5km]

Return from PH to X roads and turn left signed Bisley. Turn right at next X roads also signed Bisley. Follow this road to T jn and turn right signed Stroud, and turn left on the way up the hill signed Bisley and back into the village. [1.8m/2.9km]


## INFORMATION

**Pubs:**  Bisley - *The Stirrup Cup and The Bear Inn*
Miserden - *The Carpenters Arms*
Daneway - *The Daneway*
Oakridge - *The Butchers Arms*

**Rail access:**  There is a station in Stroud, 3 miles away.

**Parking:**  There is limited parking in Bisley.

**Towns and Attractions:**  see pages 36 - 38.
(17) Bisley, (18) Miserden, (19) Daneway

# BISLEY, MISERDEN AND DANEWAY
## Distance: 12.4 miles / 19.8km  Terrain *** strenuous

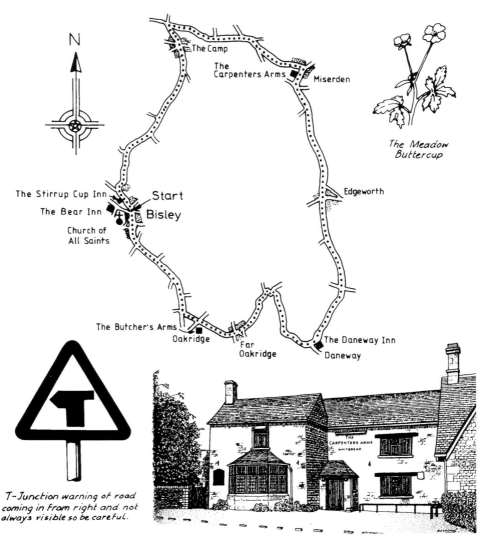

N

The Camp

The Carpenters Arms

Miserden

The Meadow Buttercup

The Stirrup Cup Inn

Start

The Bear Inn

Bisley

Church of All Saints

Edgeworth

The Butcher's Arms

Oakridge

Far Oakridge

The Daneway Inn

Daneway

T-Junction warning of road coming in from right and not always visible so be careful.

The Carpenters Arms in Miserden

░░░░░ Built-up Area

⌇⌇ Metalled Road or Lane

•••••• Rider's Track

REARDON ©

This Drawing is Not to Scale

# BEECHPIKE, THE DUNTISBOURNES AND DAGLINGWORTH
## Distance:  15.6m / 25.1km    Terrain *** strenuous

This is a delightful undulating ride on quiet lanes with fords and churches to visit.  A most pleasing feature is the Dunt valley where you can cycle through the ford in each of the villages - a perfect entertainment for a summer's day. The ride passes some of the most beautiful churches in the Cotswolds, all worth visiting.

From The Highwayman at Beechpike go south west along the lane to Winstone. Turn right at X roads in Winstone signed Sapperton, and along this road for 2m to Jackbarrow Farm; turn left signed 'Duntisbourne Abbots 1'. On the outskirts of the village keep straight on signed Birdlip; then turn right down into Duntisbourne Abbots. [3.8m/6.1km]

At the bottom of the hill turn right signed 'Ford'. You can cycle through the ford - but it's a long way!, or go along the footpath. At the next T junction turn left to Duntisbourne Leer ford, then return up the hill and turn left signed/to Middle Duntisbourne. At Middle Duntisbourne turn left down a steep hill to the ford, then return up hill and turn left signed Duntisbourne Rouse (20): you will pass the Saxon church on the left. Continue down the valley to T junction in Daglingworth (21) and turn left into the village, and turn right at X roads up to the church. [2.5m/4km]

Return to X roads and straight over signed Perrott's Brook, and up a short steep hill, and to A417 roundabouts and underpass. Straight over both roundabouts signed Perrott's Brook, and follow the lane to The Bear on A435. [2m/3.2km]

From The Bear return a very short way up the hill and turn right signed Bagendon, and then left at first junction also signed Bagendon. Go straight through Bagendon and up the hill out of the village. At the next T junction turn left and as you come into Woodmancote bear left at the junction signed Rapsgate, and follow the road through the village and leave along Robinson Lane. 2.6m/4.2km]

After 1.3m at Y junction keep left signed Elkstone; and at next X roads turn sharp left signed Beechpike, and across the valley and up the other side and pass the PYO fruit farm on the left. At junction turn left, under A417 underpass, left at junction at far side, and back to The Highwayman at Beechpike.  [4.7m/7.6km]

## INFORMATION
**Pubs:**  North of Winstone - *The Highwayman*  On A435 - *The Bear*
**Parking:**  There is limited parking near Beechpike.
**Towns and Attractions:** see pages 36 - 38. (20) Duntisbourn (21) Daglingworth

# BEECHPIKE, THE DUNTISBOURNES AND DAGLINGWORTH
## Distance: 15.6m / 25.1km    Terrain *** strenuous

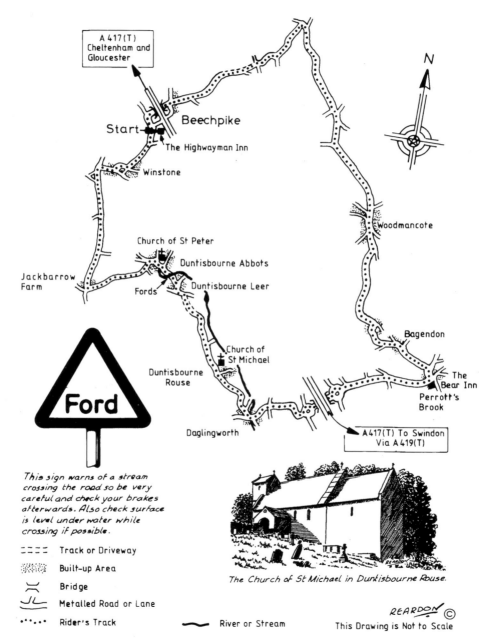

A 417(T)
Cheltenham and
Gloucester

N

Start

Beechpike

The Highwayman Inn

Winstone

Woodmancote

Church of St Peter

Duntisbourne Abbots

Jackbarrow
Farm

Duntisbourne Leer

Fords

Bagendon

Church of
St Michael

The
Bear Inn

Duntisbourne
Rouse

Perrott's
Brook

Daglingworth

A417(T) To Swindon
Via A 419(T)

**Ford**

This sign warns of a stream
crossing the road so be very
careful and check your brakes
afterwards. Also check surface
is level under water while
crossing if possible.

⌐⌐⌐⌐  Track or Driveway

▨▨▨▨  Built-up Area

≍  Bridge

⊿∟  Metalled Road or Lane

•••••  Rider's Track

━━  River or Stream

The Church of St Michael in Duntisbourne Rouse.

REARDON ©
This Drawing is Not to Scale

# FAIRFORD, THE EASTLEACHES AND COLN ST. ALDWYNS
## Distance:  13.2 miles / 21.1 km   Terrain ** moderate

This gently undulating ride starts in Fairford and goes north-east through Southrop to the Eastleaches and their churches.  The ride returns through Coln St. Aldwyns and Quenington, crossing the River Coln in both villages.

Leave Fairford (22) along A417 towards Lechlade, and just outside the town turn left signed Southrop (ignore the first left turn signed Hatherop).  Through Southrop (23) and just over the River Leach turn left signed Fyfield, and follow this road through Fyfield signed Eastleach. As you enter the Eastleaches (24) one church is on the left and the other ahead, and it is worth walking along the stone footpath across and by the river. [5.4m/8.6km]

Turn left through the Eastleaches, and straight on signed Hatherop. Turn  left at first T junction, then right, both signed Hatherop. After 2.1m turn right signed Hatherop, and then left through Hatherop signed Coln St. Aldwyns, and past the River Coln to Coln St. Aldwyns. [4.5m/7.2km]

Turn left at X roads in Coln St. Aldwyns (25), and through the village. Over the River Coln and up the hill to Quenington, and at the green bear left into Quenington village (26).  Through the village with the church on your right, over the Coln again, up the hill and follow this lane back to Fairford. As you come into Fairford turn right signed Poulton back to the church and the car park. [3.3m/5.3km]


## INFORMATION

**Pubs:**  Fairford - *The Plough Inn*
Southrop - *The Swan*
Eastleach - *The Victoria Inn*
Coln St. Aldwyn - *The New Inn*
Quenington - *The Keepers Arms*

**Parking**:  There is a free car park behind Fairford Church.

**Towns and Attractions:**  see pages 36 - 38.
(22) Fairford, (23) Southrop,
(24) Eastleach Martin and Eastleach Turville,
(25) Ciln St. Aldwyns, (26) Quinington

# FAIRFORD, THE EASTLEACHES AND COLN ST. ALDWYNS
## Distance:  13.2 miles / 21.1 km   Terrain ** moderate

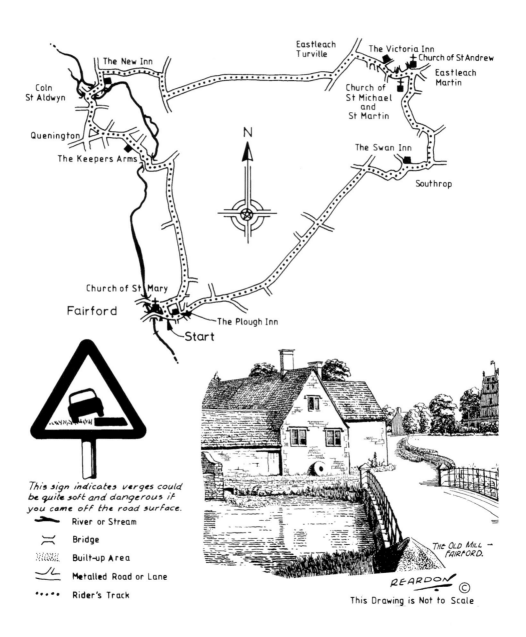

The New Inn

Eastleach
Turville

The Victoria Inn
Church of St Andrew

Eastleach
Martin

Coln
St Aldwyn

Church of
St Michael
and
St Martin

N

Quenington

The Keepers Arms

The Swan Inn

Southrop

Church of St Mary

Fairford

The Plough Inn

Start

This sign indicates verges could
be quite soft and dangerous if
you came off the road surface.

〰 River or Stream

⨪ Bridge

▨ Built-up Area

⌇ Metalled Road or Lane

••••• Rider's Track

THE OLD MILL —
FAIRFORD.

REARDON ©

This Drawing is Not to Scale

- 23 -

# BIBURY, ALDSWORTH AND THE SALT WAY
## Distance: 14.4 miles / 23km  Terrain **   moderate

This ride starts in Bibury, said by William Morris to be the prettiest village in the Cotswolds. For part of its route it travels along one of the old Salt Ways - part of the journey of salt from Droitwich to the south coast. The ride is fairly strenuous.

Leave Bibury (29) on the B4425 towards Burford, and as you leave the village turn right signed Coln St. Aldwyns - this right turn is on a dangerous corner, so be careful. The last third of this next section of road is on the Salt Way. After 2.2m at the T junction on the outskirts of Coln St. Aldwyns (27) turn right into the village. [2.6m/4.1km]

Return from Coln St. Aldwyns to the junction and go straight on signed Aldsworth. After 3m at the B4425 turn right at the T junction, and then left into Aldsworth. (For the PH continue along B4425 to the pub on the left.) [3.4m/5.5km]

To leave Aldsworth take the road signed Northleach, and continue along this undulating road for 2.8m to X roads just south of Eastington. Turn left here signed Fossebridge.   [4.7m/7.5km]

At the next X roads turn left onto the Salt Way again, signed Ablington and Bibury, and along this road through Ablington back to Bibury. [3.7m/6km]

## INFORMATION

**Pubs:**   Bibury - *The Catherine Wheel*
Coln St. Aldwyns - *The New Inn*
Aldsworth - *Sherborne Arms*

**Parking:**  There is very limited parking on this route.

**Towns and Attractions:** see pages 36 - 38.
(25) Coln St. Aldwyns
(26) Bibury

# BIBURY, ALDSWORTH AND THE SALT WAY
## Distance: 14.4 miles / 23km  Terrain ** moderate

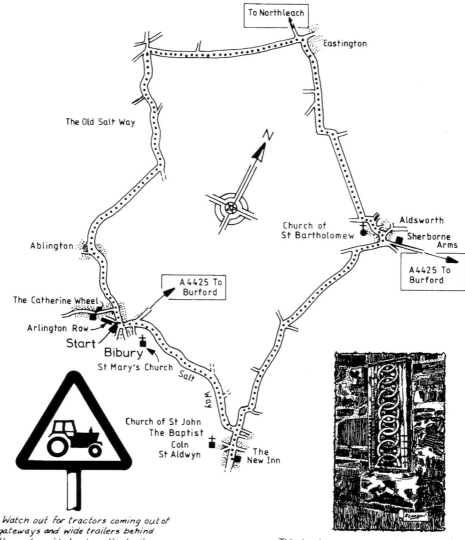

To Northleach

Eastington

The Old Salt Way

N

Church of
St Bartholomew

Aldsworth
Sherborne
Arms

Ablington

A4425 To
Burford

A4425 To
Burford

The Catherine Wheel

Arlington Row

Start

Bibury

St Mary's Church    Salt  Way

Church of St John
The Baptist
Coln
St Aldwyn

The
New Inn

*Watch out for tractors coming out of gateways and wide trailers behind them, also wide loads on the trailers which could be dangerous on narrow lanes.*

Built-up Areas

Metalled Road or Lane

•••••  Rider's Track

*This is a tombstone, not a buttress, believed to have been carved by the Vikings. It can be found in the outside North wall of the chancel of St Mary's Church in Bibury.*

REARDON ©
This Drawing is Not to Scale

# MILTON UNDER WYCHWOOD, BLEDINGTON AND THE WESTCOTES

## Distance: 13.3 miles / 21.2km Terrain ** moderate

This undulating ride starts in Milton and goes north past Bruern Wood and along a track through Foxholes. From Bledington it goes uphill through Icomb, and to the Westcotes, before coasting back to Milton.

From Milton under Wychwood take the road opposite the Quart Pot PH signed Kingham. After 1.3m turn right at T junction signed Bruern, and then the first (unsigned) left turn just before a wood. The tarmac turns to a track and there is usually a field of Jacobs sheep at Foxholes - the road will become tarmacked again. [2.9m/4.6km]

At Foscot T junction turn right, no sign, and at B4450 turn left signed Bledington. Cycle through Bledington (28) to the green which is on the far side of the village. From Bledington continue along B4450 for 0.6m, and turn left signed Icomb and follow the road into Icomb village. [3.5m/5.6km]

At Icomb War Memorial turn right and follow the road round and up the hill, and at T junction turn left signed Little Rissington and continue to A424. Turn left along A424 towards Burford, but after 0.5m turn left signed Church Westcote, and go through Church Westcote and Nether Westcote to Idbury. [3.9m/6.2km]

Turn right at Idbury T junction signed Stow, and then left signed Fifield. Cycle through Fifield and over Hill Farm Barn X roads and turn left at High Lodge Farm X roads signed Milton. Bear left at next junction signed Milton under Wychwood, and return to Milton Under Wychwood. [3m/4.8km]

## INFORMATION

**Pubs:** Milton Under Wychwood - *The Quart Pot*
Bledington - *Kings Head Inn*
Nether Westcote - *The New Inn*

**Railway** - Shipton station is only 1.5m from the start.

**Parking:** You could park in Milton Under Wychwood

**Towns and Attractions:** see pages 36 - 38.
(28) Bledington

# MILTON UNDER WYCHWOOD, BLEDINGTON AND THE WESTCOTES

## Distance: 13.3 miles / 21.2km Terrain ** moderate

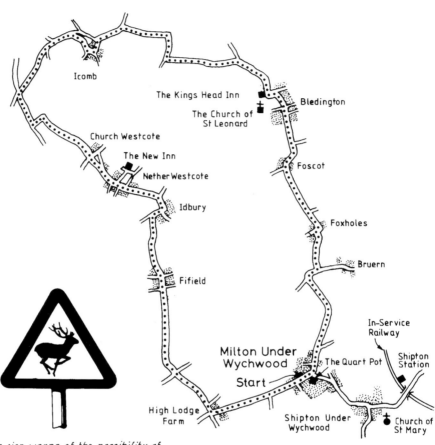

Icomb

The Kings Head Inn

The Church of St Leonard

Bledington

Church Westcote

The New Inn

Nether Westcote

Foscot

Idbury

Foxholes

Fifield

Bruern

In-Service Railway

Milton Under Wychwood

Start

The Quart Pot

Shipton Station

High Lodge Farm

Shipton Under Wychwood

Church of St Mary

*This sign warns of the possibility of fairly large wild animals suddenly running into or across the road and it could be dangerous.*

N

Built-up Areas

Metalled Road or Lane

•••••• Rider's Track

*REARDON* ©

This Drawing is Not to Scale

# STOW ON THE WOLD, THE SWELLS AND THE ODDINGTONS
### Distance:  10.5m / 16.8km  Terrain *** strenuous

The ride starts from Stow and goes down the hill to the west, and then circles the town to the north and the east. There are several attractive villages and the green at Broadwell is a good place for a picnic.

Turn left out of car park up to Stow centre (29), and at the traffic lights go more or less straight over on B4068 signed  Lower Swell.  In Lower Swell (30) turn right signed Upper Swell. After 0.8m turn right at the T junction into Upper Swell; then return, pass the T junction & take the first right signed Donnington Brewery. Pass the brewery, turn right at T junction, & then bear right, and right onto A424 signed Stow. Take the first left turn signed Donnington (31). Go straight through Donnington, then straight over A429 X roads, and bear right into Broadwell (32). [5.4m/8.6km]

From Broadwell take the road signed Oddington to the A436. At A436 turn left, and then first right into Lower Oddington (33). Turn left down a lane to the church. Return to the 'through' road, and continue through to Upper Oddington, and then on to  B4450 T junction. [3.3m/5.3km]

Turn right up B4450, and at its junction with A436 turn sharp left signed Maugersbury.  In Maugersbury turn right signed Stow up past the 'phone box and back to Stow (29). [1.8m/2.9km]

## INFORMATION

**Pubs:**  Stow - there are several pubs here.
Lower Swell - *Golden Ball*
Broadwell - *The Fox*
Lower Oddington - *Horse and Groom*
Upper Oddington - *The Fox*

**Rail access:**  You could join the ride in Broadwell which is about 5 miles from Moreton in Marsh station.

**Parking:**  Stow has a car park on the right hand side of A436 leaving Stow towards Chipping Norton.

**Towns and Attractions:** see pages 36 - 38.
(29) Stow on the Wold, (30) Lower Swell, (31) Donnington, (32) Broadwell, (33) Lower Oddington

# STOW ON THE WOLD, THE SWELLS AND THE ODDINGTONS
## Distance:  10.5m / 16.8km  Terrain *** strenuous

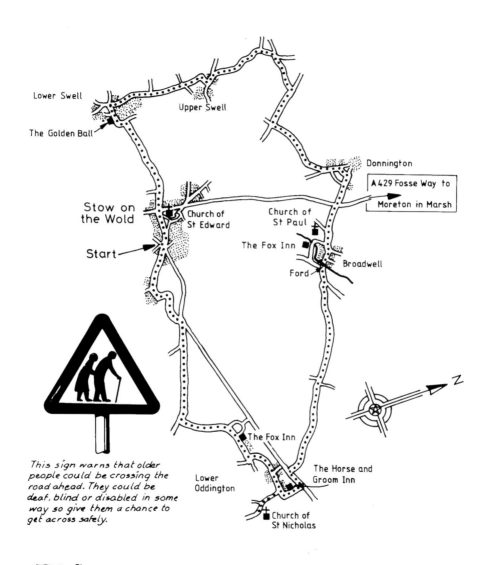

Lower Swell

Upper Swell

The Golden Ball

Stow on the Wold

Church of St Edward

Start

Donnington

A429 Fosse Way to Moreton in Marsh

Church of St Paul

The Fox Inn

Ford

Broadwell

This sign warns that older people could be crossing the road ahead. They could be deaf, blind or disabled in some way so give them a chance to get across safely.

The Fox Inn

Lower Oddington

The Horse and Groom Inn

Church of St Nicholas

Z

——— Stream

░░░ Built-up Area

⌒ Metalled Road or Lane

•••••• Rider's Track

REARDON ©

This Drawing is Not to Scale

# GUITING POWER, NAUNTON AND THE COTSWOLD FARM PARK
## Distance: 10.4 miles / 16.6 km  Terrain *** strenuous

This hilly ride starts in Guiting Power and goes through Naunton - two attractive Cotswold villages. It then goes uphill to the Farm Park, and returns across a steep valley through Kineton and back to Guiting Power.

Leave Guiting Power (34) along the road adjacent to Watson's Bakers and after 0.8m turn left at an unsigned junction. Go down the hill and up the other side to the B4008, and turn left along it. After 0.4m, just over the X roads, bear left signed Naunton. Go down to the village, over the river and follow the road through the village to the PH. [2.9m/4.6km]

Turn left just before the PH up an unsigned lane. Turn right at the top of the hill signed The Slaughters, and then at the next T junction turn left, no sign. Follow this road north for 1.9m to the Cotswold Farm Park (35) on the left. [3.2m/5.1km]

Turn left out of the Farm Park, and take the next left turn unsigned, but with a 'Ford' sign in the road. There is a steep downhill before crossing the River Windrush, and then uphill to Kineton. Go straight over X roads signed Roel Gate, and after 1.4m turn left at X roads signed Guiting Power, and back to the village. [4.3m/6.9km]


## INFORMATION

**Pubs:**  Guiting Power - *The Farmers Arms*
B4068 - *Foxhill*
Naunton - *Black Horse*
Kineton - *Halfway House*

**Parking**:  You may be able to park near the green in Guiting Power.

**Towns and Attractions:**  see pages 36 - 38.
(34) Guiting Power,
(35) Cotswold Farm Park

# GUITING POWER, NAUNTON AND THE COTSWOLD FARM PARK
## Distance: 10.4 miles / 16.6 km  Terrain *** strenuous

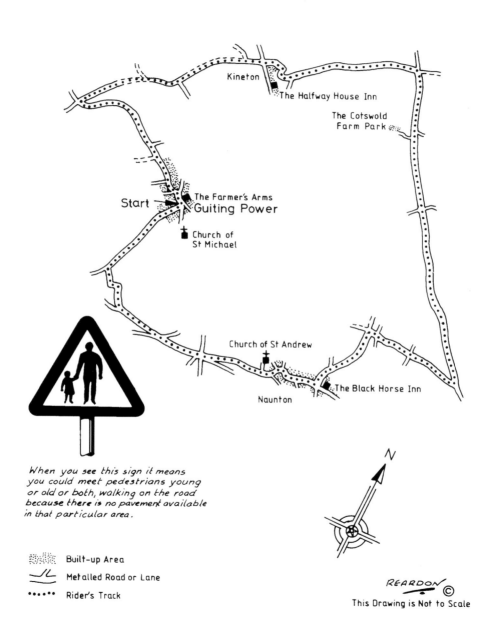

When you see this sign it means you could meet pedestrians young or old or both, walking on the road because there is no pavement available in that particular area.

Built-up Area

Metalled Road or Lane

Rider's Track

N

REARDON ©

This Drawing is Not to Scale

# KINETON AND SNOWSHILL
## Distance: 11.1 miles / 17.8km Terrain *** strenuous

This is a high, undulating ride in the north Cotswolds. The ride goes to Snowshill on the edge of the Cotswold scarp; you could visit the Manor. It crosses the River Windrush near Kineton.

From Kineton go north signed Temple Guiting, and continue up this road to B4077 near Ford. Go straight over, and continue north for 2.7m and then turn left signed Snowshill, and into Snowshill village. You could visit Snowshill Manor (36). [5.1m/8.1km]

Bear right just before Snowshill church, and at the X roads turn right signed Bourton on the Water. Go straight over the next X roads, and after 0.7m follow the road round to the right, both signed Bourton on the Water. Keep straight on along this high undulating road for 2.9m to B4077. [3.9m/6.3km]

Straight over B4077 signed Bourton, but then take first right turn after 0.9m along an unsigned road with 'Ford' sign. Go down the steep hill to the River Windrush, and up the other side, back to Kineton. [2.1m/3.4km]

## INFORMATION

**Pubs:** Snowshill - *Snowshill Arms*
Kineton - *Halfway House*

**Parking:** The villages have narrow roads and parking is very limited.

**Towns and Attractions:** see pages 36 - 38.
(36) Snowshill Manor

# KINETON AND SNOWSHILL
## Distance: 11.1 miles / 17.8km Terrain *** strenuous

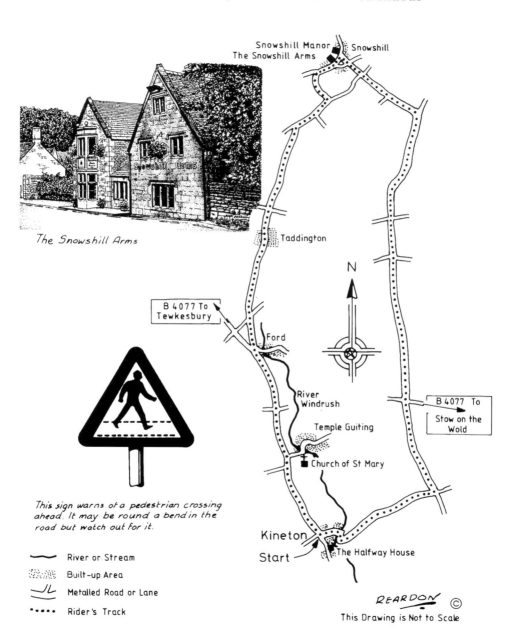

The Snowshill Arms

Snowshill Manor
The Snowshill Arms
Snowshill

Taddington

N

B 4077 To
Tewkesbury

Ford

River
Windrush

B 4077 To

Stow on the
Wold

Temple Guiting

Church of St Mary

Kineton
Start

The Halfway House

This sign warns of a pedestrian crossing ahead. It may be round a bend in the road but watch out for it.

— River or Stream

Built-up Area

Metalled Road or Lane

····· Rider's Track

REARDON ©
This Drawing is Not to Scale

# ILMINGTON, KIFTSGATE AND EBRINGTON
## Distance:  12.4 miles / 19.8km  Terrain *** strenuous

This hilly ride on the northern edge of the Cotswolds has some lovely views, and the chance of visiting both Kiftsgate and Hidcote Manor Gardens.

Leave Ilmington (37) on the road signed Mickleton and follow it for 2.4m around the bottom of the Cotswold scarp. As the road bends sharp right turn left signed Kiftsgate Gardens and ride up the hill to Kiftsgate Gardens (38) on the right. It is worth stopping on the brow of the hill to look behind at the view. (If you want to visit Hidcote Manor Gardens (39) they are to the left.) [3.9m/6.2km]

Keep straight on past Kiftsgate to X roads after 1.1m, and straight over signed Ebrington. Go straight over the next X roads also signed Ebrington, and as you come into Ebrington (40) keep straight on at the junction into the village. [2.2m/3.5km]

Follow the road through Ebrington, signed Charingworth. Go straight through Charingworth, and at the B4035 bear left (unsigned) for 0.9m. [2.8m/4.5km]

At the next X roads turn left signed Darlingscott, and follow this lane for 1.7m to a T junction. Turn left signed Ilmington, and after 1m turn left to Ilmington, and back into the village. [3.5m/5.6km]

## INFORMATION

**Pubs:**  Ebrington - *Ebrington Arms*
Ilmington - *Red Lion*

**Parking:**  You could park in Ilmington.

**Towns and Attractions:**  see pages 36 - 38.
(37) Ilmington,
(38) Kiftsgate Court Gardens,
(39) Hidcote Manor Gardens,
(40) Ebrington

# ILMINGTON, KIFTSGATE AND EBRINGTON
## Distance: 12.4 miles / 19.8km   Terrain *** strenuous

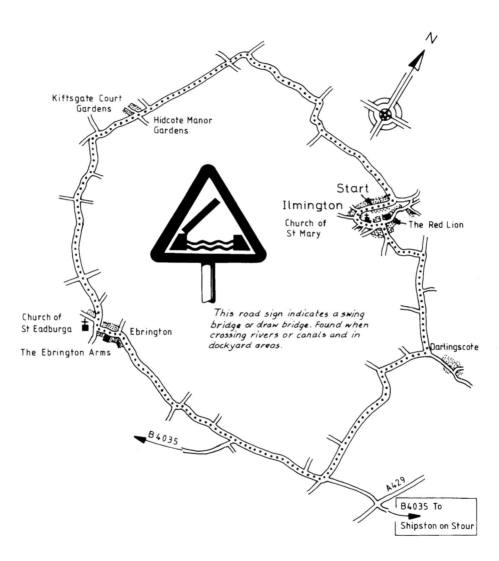

This road sign indicates a swing bridge or draw bridge. Found when crossing rivers or canals and in dockyard areas.

Kiftsgate Court Gardens

Hidcote Manor Gardens

Start
Ilmington

Church of St Mary

The Red Lion

Church of St Eadburga

Ebrington

The Ebrington Arms

Darlingscote

B4035

A429

B4035 To Shipston on Stour

Built-up Area

Metalled Road or Lane

Rider's Track

# Towns and Attractions to visit on our Cycle Rides

Ch = church   F = ford   PH = pub   Sh = shop   Ts = teas   T = toilets   M = museum

**1. SHERSTON** The town is first mentioned in 896 AD and was called 'Scorranstan' deriving from the Old English word for boundary stone - Gloucestershire and Wiltshire or the Saxon kingdoms of Mercia and Wessex. The market place in the High Street has existed since the 15th century. The church of the Holy Cross dates back to Norman times.   [Ch PH Sh]

**2. EASTON GREY** This attractive village is on the River Avon - there are pretty views from the bridge.

**3. WESTONBIRT ARBORETUM** It was founded in 1829, & contains one of the world's largest collections of trees and shrubs. Open every day.   [T Ts]

**4. LEIGHTERTON** This compact village has some pretty gardens. The largest Cotswold Stone-Age burial chamber lies to the north-east. The church has a C19th timber framed belfry. A number of American Airmen are buried in the cemetery on the outskirts of the village.   [Ch PH]

**5. OZLEWORTH CHURCH** is in the stableyard of the House and is approached across a private drive. The churchyard is circular, and the south doorway is C13th and has a striking arch with six big lobes. [Ch]

**6. SOUTH CERNEY** The church has much Norman work, and some Saxon;  its C12th woodcarving, the UK's only example, is now kept in a museum for security, but there is a replica here.  [CH PH Sh Ts]

**7. ASHTON KEYNES**  This village is on the River Thames. It is worth going into the areas behind the through road, and visiting the church.   [Ch PH]

**8. CRICKLADE**  has a small local museum. [Ch M PH Sh T Ts]

**9. GLOUCESTER AND SHARPNESS CANAL** The Canal Act was passed in 1793 and the canal took 34 years to complete.  It was the world's first Ship Canal, but although adapted for 1000 ton ships its commercial use has dwindled.

**10. THE WILDFOWL AND WETLANDS TRUST**  was founded in 1946 and works to save wetlands and conserve their wildlife.

**11. FRAMPTON ON SEVERN** has the largest village green in England. [PH Sh]

**12. The RIVER SEVERN**  is the longest British river, flowing 220 miles from its source on Plylimon to the sea. The Severn Bore  is caused by the incoming tide being constricted by the narrow banks and shallow bed causing a standing wave to surge upstream

**13. SAUL JUNCTION**  The junction of the Gloucester and Sharpness Canal and the (now closed) Thames and Severn canal.

**14. MINCHINHAMPTON** There is a 17th century Market House in the square. The church has many interesting features including a C14th central tower and a C14th font (which spent some time in a farmyard!). [Ch PH Sh T Ts]

**15. CHERINGTON** The Victorian drinking fountain on the green is  inscribed 'Let him that is athirst, come.'

**16. SAPPERTON** The village was a centre of the Cotswold Arts and Crafts movement, and Barnsley and the Gimsons lived here and are buried in the church-yard. [Ch PH]

**17. BISLEY** The valley clothiers spent their money on houses in Bisley. The church has an elaborate Norman font with fishes swimming inside, and outside there is a C12th Bonehouse. The Wells below the church have a Well dressing ceremony each May. [Ch Ph Sh]

**18. MISERDEN** The church doorways have some Saxon work, and the  manor chapel has a magnificent tomb. Misarden Park is on the edge of the village.  [CH PH Sh]

**19. DANEWAY**  The road crosses the Thames and Severn Canal - in use between 1789 and 1927. To the west the canal went down a long series of locks to Chalford.  To the east lies the western end of the 2.25m canal tunnel to Coates. [PH]

**20. DUNTISBOURNE ROUSE** The church has Saxon remains - note the herring bone masonry in the north wall. The churchyard overlooks the Dunt stream; and there is a scissor stile at the end of the path to the church.

**21. DAGLINGWORTH**  This lovely church has four Saxon wall sculptures, so smooth they look modern;  note also the tiny windows in the vestry wall. There are also interesting brass tablets in  the floor of the porch.

**22. FAIRFORD** The church is one of the Cotswold wool churches: it was built in the early C16th, and paid for by the Tame family, wealthy wool merchants. The mediaeval stained glass windows are famous; there are also lovely wood carvings, brasses & stone sculptures. [Ch PH Sh T Ts]

**23. SOUTHROP** The church has a C12th font decorated with carvings. John Keble lived in the village in the 1820s. [Ch PH]

**24. EASTLEACH MARTIN and EASTLEACH TURVILLE** Two lovely villages on opposite sides of the River Leach. There is an attractive stone footbridge over the river. The redundant Martin church has good examples of Decorated windows, and Mediaeval oak benches; the Turville church has a saddleback tower, a Norman doorway (Quenington school) and, inside, a lovely Early English chancel. [Ch PH]

**25. COLN ST. ALDWYNS** A pretty village on the river; the church has a Norman tower. [Ch PH Sh]

**26. QUENINGTON** Quenington Court has a circular dovecote, and a mediaeval gateway. The church has two elaborate Romanesque doorways (c.1150) which are worth seeing. [Ch PH]

**27. BIBURY** Arlington Row is a C17th row of weavers' cottages, and Arlington Mill a C17th corn mill with working machinery. The church has Saxon, Norman and later work, and the churchyard has well carved table tombs with 'bale' tops. [Ch M PH Sh T Ts]

**28. BLEDINGTON** The church is famous for its Perpendicular windows and its stained glass. You can picnic on the green. [PH Sh]

**29. STOW on the Wold** developed as a market town, particularly sheep, and there are many narrow alleys from the Market Square which were used to run sheep into/out of the square and count them as they emerged. The church has a handsome Perpendicular tower with a parapet and gargoyles. It is the highest town in the Cotswolds and the saying is 'Stow on the Wold where the wind blows cold'. [Ch PH Sh Ts T]

**30. LOWER SWELL** The War Memorial was designed by Sir Edwin Lutyens. [PH Ts]

**31. DONNINGTON** The royalists surrendered to the Parliamentarians here at the end of the Civil War (21.3.1646). Donnington Brewery is on the minor road north from Upper Swell.

**32. BROADWELL**  A very pretty village with a large green and fords over the river. The church has many C17th table tombs. [Ch F PH]

**33. LOWER ODDINGTON** Turn left in the village down a lane to St. Nicholas Church which has a restored mediaeval Doom Painting. [PH Sh]

**34. GUITING POWER**  The church has a fine Norman doorway. [PH Sh]

**35. COTSWOLD FARM PARK**  A comprehensive collection of rare breeds of British farm animals.  There is also a Pets Corner, farm trail and cafe. Admission charge. [T Ts]

**36. SNOWSHILL MANOR** Owned by the National Trust, with terraced gardens overlooking farmland. It has collections of  fine furniture, Samuri armour, toys and bicycles. [T Ts]

**37. ILMINGTON**  The church has 11 mice hidden in the woodwork (by Rob Thomson, the 'mouse man' of Kilburn).  The entrance and tower have Norman origins.  [Ch PH Sh]

**38. KIFTSGATE COURT GARDENS**  There are many rare shrubs & plants, & a collection of roses, including 'Kiftsgate' the largest English rose. [T Ts]

**39. HIDCOTE MANOR GARDENS** are world famous, beautiful gardens with a series of small gardens with different themes leading into each other.  It is owned by the National Trust. [T Ts]

**40. EBRINGTON**  The church is dedicated to St. Eadburgha - a Saxon saint.  It has interesting contents including wall texts at the back of the nave with St. Paul's admonitions to husbands & wives.  [Ch PH]

If you have enjoyed this book by Sheila Booth then look out for our other cycling books and maps at our on line bookshop **www.cotswoldbookshop.co.uk**

# COTSWOLD CYCLE RIDES